Cats and Carols

Lesley Anne Ivory

A BULFINCH PRESS BOOK
LITTLE, BROWN AND COMPANY
BOSTON • NEW YORK • TORONTO • LONDON

While Shepherds Watched their Flocks by Night

Attributed to Nahum Tate (1652–1715)

WHILE shepherds watched their flocks by night,
All seated on the ground,
The angel of the Lord came down,
And glory shone around.

"Fear not", said he (for mighty dread
Had seized their troubled mind),
"Glad tidings of great joy I bring
To you and all mankind.

"To you in David's town this day
Is born of David's line
The Saviour, who is Christ the Lord;
And this shall be the sign:

"The heavenly Babe you there shall find
To human view displayed,
All meanly wrapped in swathing bands,
And in a manger laid."

Thus spake the seraph; and forthwith
Appeared a shining throng
Of angels, praising God, who thus
Addressed their joyful song:

"All glory be to God on high,
And to the earth be peace;
Good will henceforth from heaven to men
Begin and never cease."

OCTOPUSSY AND MOTLEY

LESLEY

4653

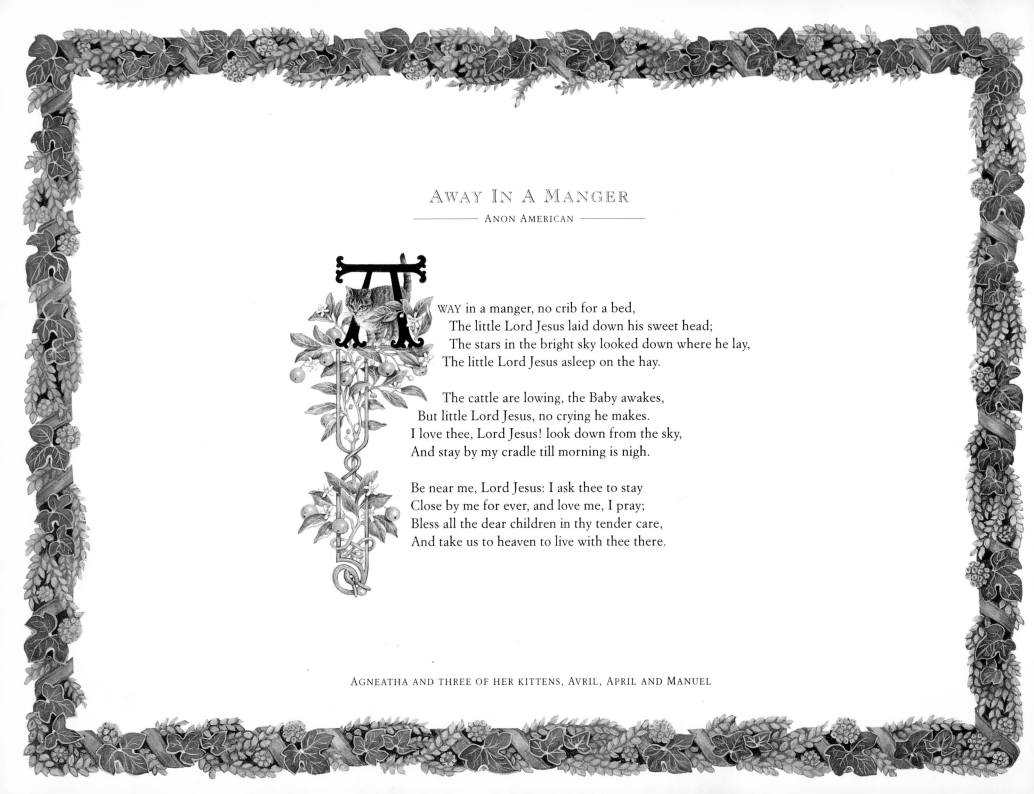

Away In A Manger

— Anon American —

WAY in a manger, no crib for a bed,
　　The little Lord Jesus laid down his sweet head;
　　The stars in the bright sky looked down where he lay,
The little Lord Jesus asleep on the hay.

　　The cattle are lowing, the Baby awakes,
　But little Lord Jesus, no crying he makes.
I love thee, Lord Jesus! look down from the sky,
And stay by my cradle till morning is nigh.

Be near me, Lord Jesus: I ask thee to stay
Close by me for ever, and love me, I pray;
Bless all the dear children in thy tender care,
And take us to heaven to live with thee there.

Agneatha and three of her kittens, Avril, April and Manuel

THREE KINGS OF ORIENT

JOHN HENRY HOPKINS (1820–91)

WE three kings of Orient are,
    Bearing gifts we traverse afar,
    Field and fountain, moor and mountain,
    Following yonder star.

    O Star of Wonder, Star of Night
    Star with royal beauty bright,
    Westward leading, still proceeding,
    Guide us to thy perfect light.

Born a king on Bethlehem plain,
Gold I bring to crown him again,
    King for ever, ceasing never
    Over us all to reign.

    O Star of Wonder, Star of Night
    Star with royal beauty bright,
    Westward leading, still proceeding,
    Guide us to thy perfect light.

Frankincense to offer have I,
Incense owns a Deity nigh;
Prayer and praising all men raising,
Worship him, God on high.

O Star of Wonder, Star of Night
Star with royal beauty bright,
Westward leading, still proceeding,
Guide us to thy perfect light.

Myrrh is mine; its bitter perfume
Breathes a life of gathering gloom;
Sorrowing, sighing, bleeding, dying,
Sealed in the stone-cold tomb.

O Star of Wonder, Star of Night
Star with royal beauty bright,
Westward leading, still proceeding,
Guide us to thy perfect light.

Glorious now behold him arise,
King, and God, and sacrifice.
Heaven sing: "Alleluia";
"Alleluia" the earth replies.

O Star of Wonder, Star of Night
Star with royal beauty bright,
Westward leading, still proceeding,
Guide us to thy perfect light.

RaRa, Twiglet and Gabrielle

Hark! The Herald Angels Sing

CHARLES WESLEY (1707–88)

HARK! the herald angels sing:
"Glory to the new-born King!
Peace on earth and mercy mild,
God and sinners reconciled!"
Joyful, all ye nations rise!
Join the triumph of the skies!
Universal Nature say:
"Christ the Lord is born today!"

Hark! the herald angels sing:
"Glory to the new-born King!"

Christ, by highest heaven adored,
Christ the everlasting Lord:
Late in time behold him come,
Offspring of a Virgin's womb.
Veiled in flesh the Godhead see!
Hail the incarnate Deity,
Pleased as man with man to dwell:
Jesus, our Emmanuel!

Hark! the herald angels sing:
"Glory to the new-born King!"

Come, Desire of Nations, come:
Fix in us thy humble home!
Rise, the Woman's conquering Seed,
Bruise in us the Serpent's head!
Adam's likeness, Lord efface:
Stamp thy image in its place!
Second Adam, from above,
Reinstate us in thy love!

Hark! the herald angels sing:
"Glory to the new-born King!"

Mild, he lays his glory by,
Born that man no more may die,
Born to raise the sons of earth,
Born to give them second birth.
Hail the heaven-born Prince of Peace!
Hail the Sun of Righteousness!
Light and life to all he brings,
Risen with healing in his wings.

Hark! the herald angels sing:
"Glory to the new-born King!"

DANDELION

O Little Town of Bethlehem

Phillips Brooks (1835–93)

O LITTLE town of Bethlehem,
How still we see thee lie!
Above thy deep and dreamless sleep
The silent stars go by.
Yet in thy dark streets shineth
The everlasting Light:
The hopes and fears of all the years
Are met in thee tonight.

O morning stars, together
Proclaim the holy Birth!
And praises sing to God the King,
And peace to men on earth;
For Christ is born of Mary,
And, gathered all above,
While mortals sleep, the angels keep
Their watch of wondering love.

How silently, how silently
The wondrous gift is given!
So God imparts to human hearts
The blessings of his heaven.

No ear may hear his coming,
But, in this world of sin,
Where meek souls will receive him, still
The dear Christ enters in.

Where children pure and happy
Pray to the blessèd Child;
Where misery cries out to thee,
Son of the mother mild;
Where Charity stands watching
And Faith holds wide the door,
The dark night wakes, the glory breaks,
And Christmas comes once more.

O holy child of Bethlehem,
Descend to us we pray;
Cast out our sin, and enter in:
Be born in us today!
We hear the Christmas angels
The great glad tidings tell;
O come to us, abide with us,
Our Lord Emmanuel!

AGNEATHA AND DANDELION

Angels We Have Heard on High

Traditional French, translated by Sir Richard Runciman Terry (1865–1938)

NGELS we have heard on high,
Singing sweetly o'er the plains,
And the mountains in reply
Echoing their joyous strains:

Gloria in excelsis Deo! Deo!

Shepherds, why this jubilee?
Why these joyous strains prolong?
What the gladsome tidings be
Which inspire your heavenly song?

Gloria in excelsis Deo! Deo!

Come to Bethlehem and see
Him whose birth the angels sing;
Come, adore on bended knee
Christ the Lord, the new-born King!

Gloria in excelsis Deo! Deo!

See him in a manger laid,
Whom the choirs of angels praise;
Mary, Joseph, lend your aid,
While our hearts in love we raise.

Gloria in excelsis Deo! Deo!

Muppet and Louise's Angel

SILENT NIGHT, HOLY NIGHT

JOSEPH MOHR (1792–1848); TRANSLATION ANON

SILENT night, Holy night,
   All is calm, all is bright;
   'Round yon virgin mother and Child,
   Holy Infant so tender and mild,
   Sleep in heavenly peace,
   Sleep in heavenly peace.

Silent night, Holy night,
  Shepherds quake at the sight;
   Glories stream from heaven afar,
    Heav'nly hosts sing Alleluia!
   Christ the Saviour is born!
   Christ the Saviour is born!

Silent night, Holy night,
Son of God, love's pure light;
Radiance beams from Thy holy face,
With the dawn of redeeming grace,
Jesus, Lord, at thy birth,
Jesus, Lord, at thy birth.

DANDELION AND THE BEAR FROM FORTNUMS

Ding! Dong! Merrily on High

G. R. Woodward (1848–1934)

Ding! Dong! merrily on high
In heav'n the bells are ringing;
Ding! Dong! verily the sky
Is riv'n with angel singing.

Gloria, Gloria! Hosanna in excelsis!

E'en so here below, below,
Let steeple bells be swungen,
And "Io, io, io!"
By priest and people sungen.

Gloria, Gloria! Hosanna in excelsis!

Pray you, dutifully prime
Your matin chime, ye ringers!
May you beautifully rime
Your evetime song, ye singers!

Gloria, Gloria! Hosanna in excelsis!

Zelly, Manuel and Dandelion

SEE, AMID THE WINTER'S SNOW

EDWARD CASWALL (1814–78)

SEE, amid the winter's snow,
  Born for us on earth below,
  See, the tender Lamb appears,
  Promised from eternal years!

Hail, thou ever blessed morn!
Hail, Redemption's happy dawn!
Sing through all Jerusalem:
"Christ is born in Bethlehem!"

Lo! within a manger lies
He who built the starry skies,
He who, throned in height sublime,
Sits amid the Cherubim.

Hail, thou ever blessed morn! etc

Say, ye holy shepherds, say:
What your joyful news today?
Wherefore have ye left your sheep
On the lonely mountain steep?

Hail, thou ever blessed morn! etc

"As we watched at dead of night,
Lo! we saw a wondrous light;
Angels, singing 'Peace on earth',
Told us of the Saviour's birth."

Hail, thou ever blessed morn! etc

Sacred Infant, all-divine,
What a tender love was thine
Thus to come from highest bliss
Down to such a world as this!

Hail, thou ever blessed morn! etc

Teach, oh teach us, holy Child,
By thy face so meek and mild,
Teach us to resemble thee
In thy sweet humility!

Hail, thou ever blessed morn! etc

MOTLEY AND THE WATERBALL

In the Bleak Mid-Winter

—— Christina Rossetti (1830–94) ——

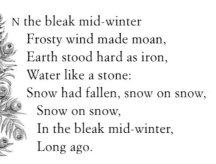

In the bleak mid-winter
  Frosty wind made moan,
  Earth stood hard as iron,
  Water like a stone:
  Snow had fallen, snow on snow,
    Snow on snow,
    In the bleak mid-winter,
    Long ago.

Our God, heaven cannot hold him
  Nor earth sustain:
    Heaven and earth shall flee away
      When he comes to reign:
      In the bleak mid-winter
    A stable place sufficed
    The Lord God almighty
    Jesus Christ.

Enough for him, whom cherubim
Worship night and day,
A breastful of milk
And a mangerful of hay:
Enough for him, whom angels
Fall down before,
The ox and ass and camel
Which adore.

What can I give him,
Poor as I am?
If I were a shepherd
I would bring a lamb;
If I were a wise man
I would do my part;
Yet what I can I give him
Give my heart,
Give, give my heart.

MALTEAZER AND THE FIRST CHRISTMAS ROSE

GOD REST YOU MERRY, GENTLEMEN

——— TRADITIONAL ENGLISH ———

OD rest you merry, gentlemen,
Let nothing you dismay,
For Jesus Christ, our Saviour,
Was born upon this day
To save us all from Satan's power
When we were gone astray.

O tidings of comfort and joy, comfort and joy,
O tidings of comfort and joy!

In Bethlehem in Jewry
This blessèd Babe was born,
And laid within a manger
Upon this blessèd morn;
The which his mother Mary
Nothing did take in scorn.

O tidings of comfort and joy, comfort and joy,
O tidings of comfort and joy!

From God our heavenly Father
A blessèd angel came,
And unto certain shepherds

Brought tidings of the same,
How that in Bethlehem was born
The Son of God by name.

O tidings of comfort and joy, comfort and joy,
O tidings of comfort and joy!

"Fear not," then said the angel,
"Let nothing you affright;
This day is born a Saviour
Of virtue, power and might,
So frequently to vanquish all
The friends of Satan quite."

O tidings of comfort and joy, comfort and joy,
O tidings of comfort and joy!

The shepherds at those tidings
Rejoicèd much in mind,
And left their flocks a-feeding
In tempest, storm and wind,
And went to Bethlehem straightaway
This blessèd Babe to find.

O tidings of comfort and joy, comfort and joy,
O tidings of comfort and joy!

But when to Bethlehem they came,
Whereat this Infant lay,
They found him in a manger
Where oxen feed on hay;
His mother Mary, kneeling,
Unto the Lord did pray.

O tidings of comfort and joy, comfort and joy,
O tidings of comfort and joy!

Now to the Lord sing praises,
All you within this place,
And with true love and brotherhood
Each other now embrace.
The holy tide of Christmas
All others doth efface.

O tidings of comfort and joy, comfort and joy,
O tidings of comfort and joy!

RaRa and Ruskin

It Came Upon the Midnight Clear

Edmund H. Sears (1810–76)

It came upon the midnight clear,
 That glorious song of old,
  From angels, bending near the earth
  To touch their harps of gold:
  "Peace on the earth, goodwill to men
   From heaven's all gracious King!"
   The world in solemn stillness lay
   To hear the angels sing.

Still through the cloven skies they come,
 With peaceful wings unfurled,
  And still their heavenly music floats,
  O'er all the weary world:
  Above its sad and lowly plains
  They bend on hovering wing,
 And ever o'er its Babel sounds
  The blessèd angels sing.

Yet with the woes of sin and strife
The world has suffered long:
Beneath the angels' strain have rolled
Two thousand years of wrong,

And man, at war with man, hears not
The love-song which they bring:
O hush the noise, ye men of strife,
And hear the angels sing!

And ye, beneath life's crushing load,
Whose forms are bending low,
Who toil along the climbing way
With painful steps and slow,
Look now! for glad and golden hours
Come swiftly on the wing;
O rest beside the weary road,
And hear the angels sing!

For lo! the days are hastening on,
By prophet-bards foretold,
When, with the ever-circling years,
Comes round the Age of Gold,
When peace shall over all the earth
Its ancient splendours fling,
And the whole world give back the song
Which now the angels sing.

ANGEL

O Come, All ye Faithful

Anon and Abbé E.J.F. Borderies (1764–1832); translated by Frederick
Oakeley (1802–80) and W.T. Brooke (1848–1917)

O Come, all ye faithful,
  Joyful and triumphant,
  O come ye, O come ye, to Bethlehem!
Come and behold him,
  Born the King of Angels!

O come, let us adore him!
  O come, let us adore him!
O come, let us adore him, Christ the Lord!
  Come and behold him,
    Born the King of Angels!
    O come, let us adore him!
    O come, let us adore him!
  O come, let us adore him, Christ the Lord!

God of God,
Light of Light,
Lo! he abhors not the Virgin's womb;
Very God,
Begotten, not created.

O come, let us adore him! etc

See how the shepherds
Summoned to his cradle,
Leaving their flocks, draw nigh to gaze!
We, too, will thither
Bend our hearts' oblations.

O come, let us adore him! etc

Lo, star-led chieftains,
Magi, Christ adoring,
Offer him incense, gold and myrrh;
We to the Christ-child
Bring our hearts' oblations.

O come, let us adore him! etc

Child, for us sinners,
Poor and in the manger,
Fain we embrace thee with love and awe;
Who would not love thee,
Loving us so dearly?

O come, let us adore him! etc

Sing, choirs of angels!
Sing in exultation!
Sing, all ye citizens of heaven above:
"Glory to God
In the highest."

O come, let us adore him! etc

Yea, Lord, we greet thee,
Born this happy morning;
Jesu, to thee be glory given,
Word of the Father
Now in flesh appearing.

O come, let us adore him! etc

OCTOPUSSY AND THE REINDEER

Good King Wenceslas Looked Out

John Mason Neale (1818–66)

GOOD King Wenceslas looked out
  On the feast of Stephen,
    When the snow lay round about,
    Deep and crisp and even;
     Brightly shone the moon that night,
     Though the frost was cruel,
      When a poor man came in sight,
Gath'ring winter fuel.

"Hither, page, and stand by me;
 If thou know'st it, telling –
  Yonder peasant, who is he?
  Where and what his dwelling?"
 "Sire, he lives a good league hence,
Underneath the mountain,
Right against the forest fence,
By Saint Agnes' fountain."

"Bring me flesh, and bring me wine!
 Bring me pine logs hither!
 Thou and I will see him dine
When we bear them thither."

Page and monarch forth they went,
Forth they went together,
Through the rude wind's wild lament
And the bitter weather.

"Sire, the night is darker now,
And the wind blows stronger;
Fails my heart, I know not how,
I can go no longer."
"Mark my footsteps, good my page,
Tread thou in them boldly:
Thou shalt find the winter's rage
Freeze thy blood less coldly."

In his master's steps he trod,
Where the snow lay dinted;
Heat was in the very sod
Which the saint had printed.
Therefore, Christian men, be sure,
Wealth or rank possessing,
Ye who now will bless the poor
Shall yourselves find blessing.

CHRISTIE AND CHESTERTON

WE WISH YOU A MERRY CHRISTMAS

TRADITIONAL ENGLISH

WE wish you a merry Christmas,
We wish you a merry Christmas,
We wish you a merry Christmas
And a happy new year!

Glad tidings we bring
To you and your kin:
We wish you a merry Christmas
And a happy new year!

Now bring us some figgy pudding,
Now bring us some figgy pudding,
    Now bring us some figgy pudding,
    And bring it us here!

Glad tidings we bring
To you and your kin:
We wish you a merry Christmas
And a happy new year!

O we won't go until we've got some,
No, we won't go until we've got some,
We won't go until we've got some,
So give it us here!

Glad tidings we bring
To you and your kin:
We wish you a merry Christmas
And a happy new year!

O we all like figgy pudding,
Yes, we all like figgy pudding,
We all like figgy pudding,
So bring it out here!

Glad tidings we bring
To you and your kin:
We wish you a merry Christmas
And a happy new year!

DANDELION AND DELABOLE WITH WYN'S SNOW-CAT

To Pauline and Chris, and Margaret, with love

Illustrations copyright © 1995 by Lesley Anne Ivory
Licensed by Copyrights

First Edition

ISBN 0-8212-2136-1

Library of Congress Catalog Card Number 94-79573
A CIP catalogue for this book is available
from the British Library

Conceived, edited and designed by Ash and Higton

Published simultaneously in the United States of America
by Bulfinch Press, an imprint and trademark of
Little, Brown and Company (Inc.),
in Great Britain by Little, Brown and Company (UK)
and in Canada by Little, Brown & Company (Canada) Limited

PRINTED AND BOUND IN BELGIUM